Tom & Clem

Ste[...]nett was born in Kent. Since graduating in
Dr[...] from Manchester University in 1968, he has been
an actor. *Tom & Clem* is his first full-length play.

STEPHEN CHURCHETT

Tom & Clem

faber and faber
LONDON · BOSTON

First published in 1997
by Faber and Faber Limited
3 Queen Square London WC1N 3AU

Photoset by Parker Typesetting Service, Leicester
Printed in England by Mackays of Chatham plc, Chatham, Kent

© Stephen Churchett, 1997

Stephen Churchett is hereby identified as author of this
work in accordance with Section 77 of the Copyright,
Designs and Patents Act 1988

A CIP record for this book
is available from the British Library
ISBN 0-571-19178-9

2 4 6 8 10 9 7 5 3 1

For my parents

Author's Note

The imagined events of this play take place against the background of history. In a few instances, I have exercised the dramatist's right to re-invent that history.

'England Arise!' (words and music by Edward Carpenter) appears in *Chants of Labour: A Songbook for the People*, published by George Allen & Unwin.

Extract from Tom Driberg's *Ruling Passions*, published by Jonathan Cape, used by permission of the Estate of Tom Driberg.

Characters

Alexei
Kitty
Tom
Clem

Tom & Clem had its first performance at the
Yvonne Arnaud Theatre, Guildford, on 25 March 1997,
presented by Michael Codron, and subsequently opened
at the Aldwych Theatre, London, on 14 April 1997. The
cast was as follows:

Alexei Daniel de la Falaise
Kitty Sarah Woodward
Tom Michael Gambon
Clem Alec McCowen

Director Richard Wilson
Designer Rob Howell
Lighting Designer Mick Hughes
Sound Designer John A. Leonard

Act One

A large room in the Cecilienhof Palace, Potsdam, Germany, 1945. An afternoon in July. A couple of small tables. Several chairs, some stacked, some scattered about the room. A telephone. A teleprinter. Some photographic floodlamps on stands. The odd cardboard box. Paperwork is scattered both on the small tables and on a long table covered with a baize tablecloth which stands upstage, and above which are suspended three large portraits in the Socialist Realist style: Josef Stalin, Harry S. Truman, and Winston Churchill. Churchill is hanging askew, one of his supporting wires having been detached. A step ladder stands near by. Through an open door we hear voices. They're speaking Russian.

Alexei (*off*) Осторожно! [Careful!]

Kitty (*off*) Ты повернись. Вот так. [You move round. That's it.]

Two uniformed figures, Kitty (mid-thirties, a second officer in the WRNS) and Alexei (mid-twenties, a Red army captain) carry in another, identically sized portrait whose subject is as yet invisible to us. They lean the new portrait against the table.

Kitty Прислони его к столу. [Lean it against the table.]

Alexei Ну, вот. Теперь давай отрежем эту проволоку. Ну, вот эти сойдут. [Here, now let's get this free. These should do it.]

He produces a pair of pliers, goes up the steps and works on releasing the remaining wire from Churchill.

Kitty supports the free-hanging side of the portrait from below.

Kitty Так пучше? [Is that better?]

Alexei Да. Почти готово. Ну, вот и всё. [Yes, almost there. That's it.]

Kitty Хорошо. Опускай медленно. [Good. Let it down slowly.]

Alexei Держишь? [Got it?]

Kitty Да. Нет. Осторожно! [Yes. No. Careful!]

Alexei Ты в порядке? [Are you all right?]

Kitty Мѐдпѐнно. Подожди пока я возьму его как спедует. [Slowly. Wait until I've got it properly.]

Alexei Я ничего не вижу. Скажи, когда ты будешь готова. [I can't see. Tell me when you're ready.]

Kitty Да. [Yes.]

Alexei releases the portrait and it slips through Kitty's hands.

Kitty Buggeration, I've broken a nail.

Alexei Ты ушиблась? [Are you hurt?]

Kitty Просто ноготь сломала. [Just a nail.]

Alexei Sorry. But you say 'yes', yes?

Kitty No, I said 'Yes, I'll tell you when I'm ready.' 'Да, Я скажу тебе, когда я буду готова.' ['Yes, I'll tell you when I'm ready.']

Alexei Ah, sorry. But no hurt?

Kitty No, it's just annoying. Ну давай. [Come on.]

They pick up Churchill, take him to the table, and then

2

start to hang the other portrait. As they do, we will see that it is Clement Atlee.

Alexei Почєму Черчиль проиграл? Что случилось? [Why did Churchill lose? What went wrong?]

Kitty Ничєго. [Nothing.] Nothing went wrong, Alexei, I've told you. It was a general election. Oh, I see. The penny's just dropped.

Alexei Please?

Kitty Uncle Joe would have assumed Mr Churchill could fix the result.

Alexei Who?

Kitty *(indicating the Stalin portrait)* Our glorious ally.

Alexei No uncle. He is father. To all people at . . . in Soviet Union.

Kitty Yes, super. Wizard. Ну давай. Я не могу держать зто вечно. [Do come on, I can't hold this for ever.]

Alexei Yes, yes, I do it. But why to change?

Kitty People wanted somebody different.

Alexei But Churchill good leader. Big help to us to win war.

Kitty I think we can agree he did his bit.

Alexei Please?

Kitty Nothing.

Alexei New leader is different man? . . . Нет, другой тип Человека? [. . . no, different *type* of man?]

Kitty Different *type* of man? Lord, yes. Chalk and cheese.

Alexei Please?

Tom enters (forty years old, wearing the uniform of a war correspondent and carrying a briefcase).

Tom I hope he's dry, Kitty.

Kitty Tom! Only just, actually.

Tom sees the front of the portrait and bursts out laughing.

Tom Oh, my giddy aunt. They said you were in here. I simply had to see. Oh, it's hilarious. I mean, Socialist Realist art makes anyone look like a hero – that's its point. Mannish girls on tractors in sun-drenched cornfields, and those charming young soldiers, rifle in hand and a sinewy arm round a wounded comrade. But I'm sorry, he still looks like my bloody dentist.

Kitty When did you get back?

Tom This morning. I managed to get a lift with some rather jolly GIs. Big black ones, Kitty. You'd love them.

Kitty Don't you think about anything else?

Alexei Можешь уже отпустить. [You can let go now.]

Kitty Ты уверен? [Are you sure?]

Alexei Да. Всё в порядке. [Yes, it's fine.]

Kitty releases her hold on the Attlee portrait. Alexei makes some fine adjustments before coming down the steps.

Kitty How was the camp?

Tom Pretty bloody grim.

He opens his briefcase and produces a bottle.

Have you any glasses?

Kitty What is it?

Tom Schnapps. Rather a good one according to the old crone who sold it to me. Extraordinary – she was living in the cellar of what remained of a very grand house that had been bombed to buggery. Absolutely batty, surrounded by stacks of film canisters and posters.

Kitty This used to be the German Hollywood, you know, Potsdam.

Tom I thought she reminded me of someone: Nosferatu.

Alexei Ну что? Будем Черчиля выносить? [Shall we take out Churchill now?]

Tom Kitty?

Kitty Of course, how rude of me! Alexei, may I present Tom Driberg, a journalist from England . . .

Tom And?

Kitty And what? Oh Lord, Tom, I'm sorry. Congratulations. It went right out of my head. Tom is not only a journalist, Alexei, but as of last Thursday, an MP. Член Парламєнта. [A Member of Parliament.]

Alexei Hallo, Tom.

Kitty Captain Alexei Prisypkin, my opposite number in the Russian delegation.

Tom Hugely pleased to meet you.

Alexei You wish drink, yes? I bring, er . . .

Kitty Glasses. Would you? You're an angel.

Tom And one for yourself.

Alexei Please?

Tom You must drink with us. We shall drink a toast to Socialism in both our great countries.

Alexei You are Socialist?

Tom Very much so, Alexei.

Alexei Ah, with him?

He indicates the Attlee portrait.

Tom Yes, Clementine Clam.

Alexei Clam?

Kitty Er . . . Устрица. [Oyster.] No, that's 'oyster'. Сорт креветки, с очень плотно закрытой раковиной. [A sort of shellfish with a very tight-shutting shell.]

Alexei Молюск? [Clam?]

Kitty Да, да. Молюск. [Yes, yes, clam.] It means he's rather laconic. Er, 'laconic' . . .

Tom He never uses one word where none will do.

Alexei I bring glasses.

He exits. Kitty begins tidying up the room, gathering papers and unstacking some chairs.

Tom How very handsome. A credit to Mother Russia.

Kitty Engaged, Tom. NATB . . . not available to buggers.

Tom I am *not* a bugger. I have a predilection for a specific act, as I've told you before, which does not actually involve . . .

Kitty Tom, don't be pedantic. I may be unshockable, but I can be bored.

Tom Nijinsky, I'm told, could do it for himself. Extraordinarily supple body, and a *membrum virile* of more than average length.

Kitty I'm not listening.

Tom Rather selfish of him if you ask me.

Kitty Tell me about the election. *What* was your majority?

Tom Seven thousand seven hundred and twenty-seven. Bloody healthy, don't you think? I seem to remember a certain second officer expressing considerable scepticism about my chances.

Kitty Oh, not about yours, no. I thought you'd get in. But I was a mite doubtful that people would kick out the old man, just because the war's over.

Tom It's not yet.

Kitty Well, Japan, yes. Here, I meant.

Tom You were 'a mite doubtful'? I recall a briefing in this very room when I asked if you had a replacement portrait ready. You nearly wet your drawers laughing.

Kitty Graphic, and rather overstated. I wasn't alone, anyway. Half the room was hooting.

Tom Yes, weren't they just? I can't wait to rub their noses in it. A hundred and forty bloody six overall majority.

Kitty I was surprised, I admit.

Tom How does it feel to be on the losing side?

Kitty Don't assume so much, Tom.

Tom What do you mean?

Kitty You think you're such a good judge of character, don't you?

Tom You don't mean you voted for us?

Kitty Yes. Lots of us did. That's why you won.

Tom My dear Kitty, I'm delighted. And somewhat astounded.

Kitty I rather surprised myself. Let alone the hooting hacks.

Tom Where the bloody hell are they all, by the way? The place is deserted.

Kitty Gone to Berlin for a last fling before we go back into formal session.

Tom When's that?

Kitty Not until tomorrow afternoon.

Tom Lucky for them. They can sleep it off after roaring and whoring their way through the rubble.

Kitty I'd jump at the chance.

Tom Really, Kitty?

Kitty The chance of a few days off, I mean. Most of my lot got some leave during the adjournment, lucky so-and-so's. Muggins here had to stay and do all the work. Same with the Russians and the Yanks. We're all pretty browned off, I can tell you. It's impossible to find anyone to do the simplest thing.

Tom looks at the Attlee portrait.

Tom When does he arrive?

Kitty consults her watch.

Kitty Within the hour. He's seeing Mr Truman at fifteen hundred. I mean, look at all this. Alexei and I shouldn't have to do this.

Tom I'd give you a hand, but I'm feeling all in.

Kitty You haven't such a thing as a nail file, have you?

Alexei enters with three glasses on a tray.

Tom Alexei! Well done. Now, shall I be mother?

Alexei Please?

Kitty Er . . . it's too idiomatic.

Tom opens the bottle, pours schnapps into the glasses one by one and hands them round.

Tom One for you.

Kitty Tom, that's far too large. I'll be squiffy.

Tom Alexei, then. I'm sure *you* don't have a problem with size.

He hands the glass to Alexei.

Alexei Thank you, Tom.

Tom And a dainty little measure for you, Kitty. And a thumping big one for me.

He pours the other two glasses and raises his.

'We will now proceed to the establishment of Socialism.'

Tom and Alexei down their drinks in one. Kitty sips hers.

You must know who said that. Vladimir Ilyich Lenin, 1917.

Alexei Ah, Lenin.

Tom (*to Kitty*) Do you know where I last saw that? It was rather crudely scrawled on a red flag in the Charing Cross Road. VE Night. There were crowds and crowds of us, dancing and singing and occasionally fornicating, and there was this flag in the middle of it all. A couple of RAF sergeants had knocked it up. Terrific.

He offers to top up Kitty's glass. She covers it with her hand. He refills Alexei's and his own glass. Alexei looks at the Attlee portrait.

Alexei New leader is like Lenin.

9

Kitty I hope not.

Alexei Same head, no? Look.

Kitty Oh, I see. Now you mention it, yes. All he needs is the little beard. What do you think, Tom?

Tom It would take more than that. If Clem proclaimed the Revolution, it would sound like a change in the railway timetable.

He raises his glass.

Socialism!

Alexei Socialism!

Tom (*to Kitty*) Raise your glass. You said you'd voted for us.

Kitty Well, yes. We just don't want you to go too far, that's all. (*Tom is refilling his and Alexei's glasses.*) Easy, Tom.

Tom Don't go all earnest on me. Women just don't understand us, do they, Alexei?

Alexei Please?

Tom 'Bacchus' Blessings are a Treasure/ Drinking is the Soldier's Pleasure/ Rich the Treasure/ Sweet the Pleasure/ Sweet is Pleasure after Pain.' (*He and Alexei drink.*)

Kitty You're not a soldier. Pope?

Tom Dryden. (*to Alexei*) An English writer.

Alexei Ah. In my country English writers very much popular. William Shakespeare. Charles Dickens. Dorotil Sairs.

Tom Who?

Alexei Dorotil Sairs.

Tom What does he write about?

Alexei No, it is she. Is woman. About aristocrat, Lord Wyemsie.

Kitty Oh, Peter Wimsey. That's Dorothy L. Sayers.

Alexei Ah. You are sure?.

Kitty Yes. (*to Tom*) I will have a drop more, actually. It's just hitting the spot.

Tom refills the glasses.

Tom So you like literature, do you?

Alexei Yes, much.

Tom And plays? Do you go to the theatre?

Alexei Ah, theatre, yes. Is good. I live in Moscow. Much theatres. Many people like.

Tom Moscow. How wonderful! And the ballet?

Alexei Ballet? Yes, I go before war. Is beautiful.

Tom You'd never have seen Nijinsky, I suppose.

Kitty Tom, if this is leading where I think it is . . .

Tom Just doing my bit for Anglo-Soviet cultural relations. No, you'd have been too young.

Alexei Please?

Tom To see the great Nijinsky dance.

Alexei I never see, no.

Tom raises his glass.

Tom Nijinsky!

Kitty Bottoms up! (*She breaks into giggles.*) But then I suppose you'd have to, wouldn't you? Get your BTM up if you wanted to do what he could do.

Tom I'm surprised at you.

Alexei What is joke, please?

Kitty Oh Lord.

Tom Nijinsky could do something rather spectacular with his body.

Alexei 'Spectacular'? Ah, like spectacle, ballet.

Tom This wasn't actually on stage . . .

Alexei (*to Kitty*) You translate, please?

Kitty What have you got me into?

Tom Don't blame me.

Kitty Er . . . well . . . Том мне рассказывал, что Нижинский мог доставлять себе удовольствие, ну, делая что-то со своим . . . понимаешь . . . ну что оычно бы делала ето жена. [Tom told me earlier that Nijinsky could pleasure himself by doing something to his . . . you know . . . that normally his wife would do.]

Alexei Я не понимаю. [I don't understand.]

Kitty Lord. Well, then . . . er . . . oh.

Tom Don't give up. I'm enjoying this.

Kitty Он мог выполнять . . . авто минет? [He was able to perform . . . auto fellatio?]

Alexei laughs.

Alexei Is not possible.

Tom It's very possible, apparently.

Alexei Наверное, зто может быть очень удобньм, иногда. [That must be very convenient sometimes.]

Tom What did he say?

Kitty Roughly, 'nice work if you can get it'.

The phone rings. Kitty answers it.

(*to phone*) Hello? . . . Yes, speaking . . . Already? . . . Yes, of course. Five minutes? . . . yes, goodbye. (*She rings off.*) The Prime Minister's here. I have to go down. Alexei, let's at least get this out on to the landing.

Kitty and Alexei move to the Churchill portrait.

Tom How are the lines to London?

Kitty Not too bad, I think. Shall I try for you?

Tom Would you?

Kitty picks up the phone.

I don't suppose there's any chance of some food?

Alexei Food? Yes, is possible. I try.

Tom Most kind.

Kitty (*to phone*) Press room . . . Could you get me a London number? . . . er, Fleet . . . (*She looks at Tom.*)

Tom Double two two nine.

Kitty (*to phone*) Double two two nine. *Reynolds News* . . . thank you. (*She rings off.*) It's all right, there's no delay.

Tom Thank you.

Kitty and Alexei exit with the portrait. Tom opens his briefcase and takes out a notebook. He flips through it to find a page. He pours himself another drink. The phone rings. He answers.

Tom (*to phone*) Hello . . . Yes, it's for me . . . Hello? . . .

copy takers, please, it's Driberg . . . Frank, sorry about yesterday. The Yanks were trying to shunt a couple of K.O.'d tanks off the road apparently. Managed to back their bulldozer into a telegraph pole and the whole bloody lot came down. It took me an hour to get through in the first place . . . Yes, where did we get to? . . .

He reads from the notebook.

Right. New para: 'The bodies were scraggy and tiny' comma 'the flesh turning patchily green and mauve' comma 'the eyes filmed and staring with the feet sticking out stiffly at odd angles and some of the mouths fixed in an eternal scream' stop 'A tiresome little breeze blew dust from the cart into our faces' stop. New para: 'Worse than any sight or sound was the smell that overhung the whole place even after a week's intensive cleaning up' colon . . . Hello? . . . hello, Frank, are you still there? . . . Oh bugger it!

He jiggles the phone cradle and keeps the receiver to his ear. Alexei enters with a plate of bread and sausage and a knife. He also carries a few box files.

Alexei Not much, Tom. But is bread and sausage.

Tom Thank you. How sweet of you . . . (*to phone*) . . . Yes, I got cut off . . . Oh, are they? What a bore. Would you keep trying for me, please? . . . Thank you. (*He rings off.*)

He sniffs the sausage.

Alexei Is not good?

Tom Is it a bit high?

Alexei Please?

Tom Just very . . . sausagey, I suppose. Thank you.

Alexei You are well?

Tom What?

Alexei You have sad face.

Tom Tired, I think.

Alexei Ah, tired, yes. More tired since war finish? I also.

Tom Yes. Strange, isn't it? But we have to look forward, Alexei, to the future. A new epoch.

Alexei Please? Last word?

Tom Epoch. The beginning of a . . . special time . . . when important things will happen.

Alexei We drink, yes?

He pours and they toast.

Epoch!

Tom Epoch!

Alexei Tom, is not to disturb if I finish to work here?

Tom No, you carry on.

Alexei sorts through the papers to put them in the box files while Tom eats.

Alexei Is good, food?

Tom I've had worse before now. (*He laughs.*) In fact, I've had wurst before now.

Alexei Is joke?

Tom Not a very good one. Oh . . . it's too complicated.

Alexei Like Nijinsky joke?

Tom Yes.

Alexei Is not much food in Germany now. In England also?

Tom No, not as bad. Especially if you've got the money.

Alexei Ah, is . . . black market?

Tom There is that, of course. But we do have rationing. 'Rationing' . . . when people are permitted to buy only a small amount of food.

Alexei Ah, Система выдача пайков. [Rationing.] Yes.

Tom Fair shares for all. Equality of sacrifice.

Alexei Is good system.

Tom Not everything is rationed, of course. You can still stuff yourself silly on some things: grouse or quail or salmon. You can even look rather chic when you sit down to eat it, if you're prepared to make sacrifices: strip off the sheets in the second spare bedroom and take them round to that marvellous little woman who'll run up a simply divine dress out of your crêpe-de-chine. And so reasonable, my dear.

Alexei Please?

Tom I get so bloody angry with England.

Alexei You not like your country?

Tom I love it in many respects. I love the Savoy Grill, I love the gossip, I love the architecture, I love the working man, I love the Royal family, I love the cottages, and I love the *Daily Express*. I hate the idle parasites of the ruling classes, suburbia, the hypocrisy, the insufferable smugness of the bourgeoisie,and the *Daily Express*. Now why don't you sit down here and have another drink?

Alexei sits near Tom, who pours drinks.

Alexei I notice some certain contradictions in such an eclectic list.

Tom Well, naturally, that's . . . What?

Alexei Your face is a picture, Tom. I apologize.

Tom I don't understand.

Alexei I think you are a man who likes to break the rules. And now I am breaking one. My command of your language is better by a considerable extent than I am supposed to pretend to.

Tom Why pretend?

Alexei Intelligence, Tom. These damn clever Intelligence types with all their bright ideas. They think if the British and the Americans believe I don't understand so much then they will not be very on their guard. So perhaps I will hear some information of significance.

Tom And have you?

Alexei No, of course not. It's simply very crazy. But everyone thinks that because the war is finished more or less, then the time is coming again for not trusting.

Tom They're probably right.

Alexei Yes. But to me it is crazy that they think I will hear important things. And it is difficult to pretend all the time not to understand. I am tired from it. It browns me off, Tom, to be very frank.

Tom I suppose even titbits can be useful to the Intelligence chaps.

Alexei That is 'gossip'?

Tom More or less.

Alexei The only thing I have learned today is from when you told Kitty about the big Negroes, the GIs. I was surprised with Kitty for such desires. With me she behaves much like English lady, very correct.

Tom Don't say anything to her, for God's sake. She'd be mortified. She only shares these little confidences with me.

Alexei I will say nothing, of course.

Tom She's quite marvellous, you know – one of the few women I really get on with. The ones in politics are so earnest and hairy, most of them.

Alexei My lips are sealed. And please, you must keep the cat in the bag also about me.

Tom From Kitty, you mean?

Alexei Please, Tom, yes. There is much gossip here. If it is discovered I am not doing what I am ordered, it would be much trouble for me.

Tom I won't breathe a word. I'd hate to think of you ending up in a salt mine on my account.

Alexei No, no, no, it is not so bad as that. But it would be trouble for me for my work. Perhaps they stop me going to London.

Tom London?

Alexei Yes, in two months, October. I will be at our embassy as third press attaché.

Tom Congratulations.

Alexei I look forward to seeing London very much. Do you think I will like?

Tom I'm sure you'll have a wonderful time. You said you like the theatre. There'll be masses of interesting stuff going on again now.

Alexei Ah, the theatre. And of course the ballet. (*He chuckles.*)

Tom What?

Alexei Nijinsky.

Tom You knew perfectly well what we were talking about. Poor Kitty.

Alexei It was very amusing to hear her explain in Russian language.

Tom How did she do?

Alexei She used very polite translation. But I know this story from before.

Tom Do you?

Alexei Yes, Tom. It is a famous story about him. I hear it many times from friends in the Bolshoi and so on.

Tom You have friends in the ballet world?

Alexei In Moscow the ballet is for every person. Not only for lords and ladies. You are surprised, I think, that ballet dancers can want to be a friend with soldiers.

Tom It's not entirely unknown in London.

Alexei Perhaps in London we meet. You are a journalist, I am a press attaché.

Tom It doesn't have to be professionally. I could be your cultural guide, show you around. You must have my address.

He reaches into his wallet.

Alexei I would like, yes.

Tom I've run out of cards.

He turns to a blank page in his notebook. As he does so, a small folded piece of paper floats out on to the floor. He takes out a fountain pen and writes in the notebook.

Never mind. Have this.

Alexei That is a beautiful pen.

Tom A Parker. Yes, isn't it?

Alexei It is very famous, Parker.

Tom There.

He tears out the page and hands it to Alexei, who reads it.

Alexei 'Great Ormond Street'. That is where?

Tom Bloomsbury. Near the British Museum.

Alexei Ah, the British Museum, yes.

Tom I've lots of friends in Bloomsbury who'd love to meet you.

The teleprinter starts to chatter. Alexei goes to it to collect the message. Tom notices the paper that fell from his notebook. He picks it up and unfolds it. As he does so he is apparently offended by its smell. He places it deep in his briefcase, takes his handkerchief, wipes his hands, and pours another drink for Alexei and himself. Alexei tears off the teleprinter message and gives it to Tom.

Alexei Big success in Philippine Islands. For American Eighth Army.

Tom At last.

Alexei Much difficult fighting there, I think. Like your war was in Far East. Malaya, Burma and so on.

Tom Absolutely bloody.

Alexei But important for England. You must protect your empire, yes?

Tom While you were building one in Europe.

Alexei The Soviet Union does not build empire. Only responds to the legitimate aspirations of working peoples of the world.

They both burst out laughing. The phone rings.

I must finish this work.

Alexei sits behind the table and sorts papers. Tom answers the phone and opens his notebook.

Tom (*to phone*) Hello? . . . Yes, thank you . . . copy takers, Driberg . . . Frank . . . yes, I know, it's impossible, isn't it? . . . Yes, do please . . . yes, colon 'a stuffy' comma 'sweetish-sour smell' comma 'not unlike the ordinary prison smell plus death and decay' semi-colon 'a stench which seemed to seep pervadingly into every channel of our heads and cranny of our clothing' stop. (*He pauses.*) Yes, I'm still here. No stop after 'clothing'. Run straight on (*he dictates extempore*) 'and to linger in everything that one took away from the camp' stop. New para: 'It may be partly my imagination but this odour still permeates a small document folded inside my notebook' colon 'opening it just now I caught the smell which rose up physically to hit me' comma 'and at once I was back in the fearful gloom and squalor of Buchenwald' as before, stop. (*He refers back to the notebook.*) 'I think that carrion stink will always haunt me' stop. That's it . . . yes, it was, very. Goodbye, Frank. (*He rings off.*)

Alexei It was bad, yes?

Tom Beyond . . . anything.

He picks up the bottle and moves to the end of the table where Alexei is working.

Alexei No more, thank you. It is enough.

Tom Oh, do. 'Bacchus' Blessings are a Treasure / Drinking is the Soldier's Pleasure . . .'

Alexei There will be justice, Tom. A big trial for these people.

Tom Balls to that. We should put the bastards up against a wall as soon as we find them.

He pours himself a drink, watches Alexei sorting the papers, deliberately drops his pen and kicks it under the table.

Bugger, my pen. It's gone near your feet.

Alexei starts to reach down behind the table.

Tom No, I'll get it. 'Sweet is Pleasure after Pain.'

He lifts the tablecloth and disappears underneath. It's a few moments before Alexei speaks.

Alexei Tom.

Tom Yes?

Alexei That is not your Parker.

Kitty (*off*) This way, sir.

Alexei leaps up as the door opens and Kitty ushers in Clem (sixty-two years old). She carries his ministerial box.

Kitty The press room, Prime Minister. It's in a bit of a state at the moment.

We hear the sound of Tom banging his head on the table and a muffled 'Ouch'. Alexei coughs and deliberately drops a box file. He gathers it up with some others and moves swiftly to the door.

Alexei Я сейас, только отнесу их в кабинет. [I'll just take these back to the office.]

22

Kitty Куда же Том исчез? [Where's Tom disappeared to?]

Alexei Том? Я не знаю. [Tom? I don't know.]

He exits. Clem looks at the portraits one by one.

Kitty Rather good of you, sir, if I may say so.

Clem acknowledges her comment with a smile, and moves nearer the Stalin portrait.

Clem *Student Prince.*

Kitty Sir?

Clem Uniform. Very showy. Something out of operetta.

Kitty Yes, sir.

Clem Others catching us up? Where's my Mr Elyot?

Kitty He went off with the Foreign Secretary, Prime Minister, to see the Americans before your three o'clock meeting with the President.

Clem moves towards the door.

Clem Got something for him before he goes in. Lead on.

As Kitty is almost through the door, Clem following, Tom lifts the tablecloth to peer out, but immediately retreats as Clem turns and comes back into the room.

Matter of fact . . . what's the time now?

Kitty Fourteen twenty-six, sir.

Clem Got a few things to catch up on. Would I be disturbed here?

Kitty I could make sure you weren't, sir. But wouldn't you be more comfortable at your villa?

Clem Not worth it, if I'm no trouble here. My box, please.

23

He takes his box from Kitty, puts it on the table and opens it to take out a document which he gives her.

Kitty In that case I'll post someone at the end of the corridor, sir, if you need anything. And there's a telephone there.

Clem Good. Get this to Elyot, would you, before they go in? And he's to pass it to Mr Bevin.

Kitty Yes, Prime Minister.

Clem And tell Elyot where I am, of course.

Kitty Sir.

She exits. Clem takes a pipe from his pocket and lights it. He removes some documents from his box, places them to one side and brings out a book. He puts on his glasses and settles in a chair to read. Tom emerges from under the table holding aloft his pen.

Tom Eureka!

An alarmed Clem moves for the door.

Don't worry, Prime Minister, it's me – Driberg. Tom Driberg, sir.

Clem Driberg. Yes. Pleased to meet you.

Tom And I you, Prime Minister. Although I had assumed a first meeting in somewhat different circumstances.

Clem Quite. Congratulations, of course.

Tom Thank you, sir.

Clem Glad to have you on board. Dusty under there.

Tom follows Clem's gaze to his trousers and dusts off his knees.

Tom Oh thank you, Prime Minister.

Clem You're here for your paper?

Tom Yes, I arrived this morning. After . . . another assignment.

Clem Glad you're using your talents for someone on our side at last.

Tom I did have a pretty free hand at the *Express*, to give them their due.

Clem Enjoyed your column often. Shame it was for him.

Tom Lord Beaverbrook was very good to me in many ways.

Clem And was he behind Mr Churchill's election broadcast?

Tom I don't know. It did sound like him, didn't it? That we'd have to bring in some kind of Gestapo if we won. Very impish.

Clem Disgraceful. If we've got to have Tories, they should at least be gentlemen. Gift to us, of course, as it turned out. The people don't scare that easily after these last years.

Tom Indeed. Well, Prime Minister, I can see you're busy . . .

Clem Don't go. We'll talk. Sit down.

Tom Thank you, sir.

Clem First chance I've had to talk to a new chap. Sorting out the cabinet.

Tom You've picked a good team, if I may say so. Bloody good.

Clem No need for language, Driberg.

Tom Sorry, Prime Minister.

Clem How do we proceed then? Your view.

Tom Sir?

Clem To win the peace.

Tom We have to get it first, don't we? There's still the Japanese. That could drag on for months.

Clem Yes, possibly. But after?

Tom At home, you mean?

Clem Yes, yes. Foreign policy will come down to response as much as initiative, in the near future at least.

He stands up to look at Stalin and Truman.

'There's no art to find the mind's construction in the face.' More's the pity.

Tom Especially that kind of art. Too too awful.

Clem Not your cup of tea?

Tom God! No bl . . . blessed fear, no.

Clem Was a time when you were keen on all things Soviet, I understood.

Tom I assure you I know where my loyalties lie, Prime Minister.

Clem I hope so. A great task ahead of us, you know. Mustn't let the people down. No room for self-indulgence.

Tom I'm not sure I follow.

Clem First time the party has been entrusted with effective power – thumping majority, country behind us. Must pull together.

Tom Indeed. As long as it's in the right direction.

Clem Which is?

Tom Proceeding to the establishment of Socialism.

Clem Yes, yes, yes. This isn't 1917.

Tom I would venture to suggest it still holds true.

Clem Democratic Socialism.

Tom Of course. Whatever 'democratic' means.

Clem Government by discussion, that's what it means. Perfectly efficient, as long as you can stop people talking.

Tom Stop them?

Clem Always comes a point, yes – cut the cackle and get on with it. We haven't been elected to theorize . . . or to spout slogans. Leave that to the Marxians.

Tom I must confess to rather a soft spot for old Karl and his slogans. 'Workers of the world, unite.' An admirable sentiment.

Clem Someone should remind the Generalissimo. At the moment it's 'Workers of the world, divide . . . into three zones.'

Tom Is agreement near, sir?

Clem A few more days' horse trading.

Tom On Europe?

Clem Germany especially. None of us wants her too strong too soon, for obvious reasons. Leave her weak, though, and she won't be a buffer.

Tom A buffer?

Clem For us against the Russians and for the Russians against us.

Tom 'Us' being the Americans as well.

Clem We owe them a great deal.

Tom We mustn't let ourselves be steam-rollered, though, surely, Prime Minister.

Clem We'll safeguard our interests. Or as the Foreign Secretary puts it, 'We won't let Britain be barged about.'

Tom I'm sure you won't.

Clem *I'll* be taking a back seat. Don't keep a dog and bark yourself, and Mr Bevin is a real terrier.

Tom Quite, sir.

Clem And he'll be good outside the conference room, which is just as important. There's been a lot going on under the table already, especially with the Russians.

Tom suppresses a laugh.

What?

Tom Nothing. Something silly. But getting back to . . . I hold no brief for Stalin. He is still our ally, of course.

Clem Just, yes.

Tom And I don't think the mistakes . . . the excesses of one leader invalidate a political theory. That'd be throwing the baby out with the bath water.

Clem It's alien, your baby. Not British.

Tom International, surely.

Clem We have our own perfectly good traditions to call on, and they're considerably older than Marx and Lenin.

Tom Christian Socialism, Robert Owen?

Clem Sound stuff.

Tom Rather less developed?

Clem As yet.

Tom And desperately lacking . . . bravura.

Clem What's that to the point?

A knock at the door.

Come.

Kitty enters with an envelope.

Kitty Sorry to disturb you, sir, but Mr Elyot would like you to have sight of this immediately. I'm to take it back when you've finished.

Clem opens the envelope and reads the single sheet inside.

Clem Thank you. Do you know Mr Driberg?

Kitty Yes, sir.

Tom Kitty.

Kitty I was wondering where you'd got to.

Tom I'll tell you one day. Have you seen Captain . . . Alexei?

Kitty Not since he was in here, no.

Tom We had a most interesting talk.

Kitty Don't tell me – about Nijinsky.

Tom He's quite a fan. Of that sort of thing.

Kitty Really. You wouldn't think so to look at him.

Tom Life would be very dull if everything was what it seemed.

Clem writes a comment on the paper he's reading,

replaces it in the envelope and returns it to Kitty.

Clem Thank you.

Kitty Can I get you anything, Prime Minister? Some refreshment?

Clem A bit peckish. Such a thing as rice pudding?

Kitty Rice pudding, sir?

Clem And a little treacle.

Kitty I'll see what I can do. As soon as I've delivered this.

Kitty exits.

Clem So. Winning the peace.

Tom Implement our policies.

Clem Order?

Tom Sir?

Clem In what order? Priorities.

Tom Nationalization. A demonstrable Socialist response to the historic claims of the working class.

Clem Turgid jargon, if I may say so . . .

Tom Well . . .

Clem . . . especially as we've been elected by all the people, not just one class. Class won't matter so much now, you see. People have got used to working together, making common cause. We'd never have won this war if people hadn't put divisions aside and placed the public good before their own interests.

Tom We are committed to nationalization: coal, railways, electricity . . .

Clem Yes, yes, and we will have them. But not as an

article of faith. Because it's practical as well as just. The state has directed essential production for the last few years and it's worked. Even the owners have seen that, most of them.

Tom They'll try and hang on, though, won't they?

Clem Not necessarily. Industry's exhausted, bankrupt. They'll be pleased to get shot of them.

Tom That makes it sound rather painless.

Clem And if it is?

Tom Doesn't it diminish the impact? Symbolically speaking.

Clem Oh, symbols.

Tom They can be very important.

Clem More important now are practicalities. Housing, food, a health service.

Tom Of course. We want all those things. But we must be bold, must we not, Prime Minister? This is a new epoch.

Clem Don't expect Jerusalem overnight.

Tom That is still the destination, though?

Clem Of course. But we will be a station on the line, not the terminus.

Tom At least the trains will be ours.

Clem You should read more William Blake, you know, less Karl Marx.

Tom Perhaps. There is a line from Blake. Something about 'excess' and 'wisdom'.

Clem Doesn't ring a bell.

Tom Is that what you have there, sir – Blake?

Clem No, rather lighter.

Tom is about to look at Clem's book when the teleprinter starts to operate. Tom goes over to read the message.

Tom Tokyo has rejected the ultimatum.

Clem I've just been told.

Tom Oh yes, of course. You would.

Clem The wording, though?

Tom It's their Prime Minister. (*reading*) 'The Japanese Government does not consider the Potsdam Proclamation of great importance. We must ignore it. It will merely serve to re-enhance our resolve to carry the war forward unfalteringly to a successful conclusion.'

We hear the sirens of approaching vehicles.

Clem Could cost another million, they say. Casualties.

Tom If we invade?

Clem According to the Americans.

We can now hear the screeching arrival of cars and motorbikes, with whistles, doors slamming, shouting. Tom wanders to the window to look out.

That'll be Mr Truman now.

Tom Terribly smart, the Americans.

Clem Showy. Too much brouhaha.

Clem gathers the contents of his box and replaces them, but misses his book, which stays on the table.

Will I see you at the reception tonight, Driberg?

Tom I don't believe it's open to the press, sir.

Clem I'll have a word. Could be interesting for you.

Tom I'd be most grateful, Prime Minister.

Clem Something to wear, have you?

Tom I didn't bring . . . only this.

Clem Can't be helped. Sponge and press wouldn't go amiss, though.

A knock at the door.

Come.

Kitty enters carrying a tray with a bowl of rice pudding, which she places on the table.

Kitty The President has just arrived, sir.

Clem We heard.

Kitty Will you have time for this?

Clem A mouthful.

He tries the rice pudding.

Kitty (*to Tom*) I've just seen Captain Prisypkin now. He's waiting to carry on in here.

Tom Is he? I'll do my best not to get in his way then, Kitty.

Kitty I'm sure you won't.

Clem Very tasty. Lead on.

Kitty and Clem exit. Tom wanders over to the window and looks out. He is waving at someone when Alexei enters.

Alexei Well, Tom, that was a near shave.

Tom Couldn't have been nearer. Still, no harm done.

Alexei Who do you greet?

Tom Just waving at one of the GIs in the courtyard.

Alexei A Negro?

Tom Yes. Must be at least six three. Very tall.

Alexei I have never seen, before I come here. Negroes. You have some in London?

Tom Oh, yes. The night-clubs. I'll have to take you. You've heard of Soho?

Alexei Soho, yes.

Tom Frisco's. And the Shim Sham. Dancing and carrying on. You'll have a wonderful time. The Shim Sham's chock-a-block with black chaps. Huge fun. Huge everything. On which subject . . .

Tom moves towards Alexei, who retreats.

Alexei Tom.

Tom Yes?

Alexei Please, I do not offend you, I hope. But what happened before . . . when you . . . it is not really something for me, I think.

Tom Oh, I got the distinct impression, not to say *feeling*, that it was starting to be not entirely unacceptable.

Alexei I *do* offend you, I think.

Tom Not at all. Disappointed.

Alexei You see, I was not on guard. It was a surprise.

Tom Exactly. That was the fun of it.

Alexei Fun? Like joke?

Tom Not a joke, no. Fun. Exuberance. Life.

34

Alexei But I will be married soon.

Tom Congratulations.

Alexei Thank you.

Tom What's that got to do with it?

Alexei Naturally this fact must tell you that I am not a man of your kind.

Tom My dear Alexei, if I had half a crown for every man not 'of my kind' who welcomed my undoubted skill as a fellator, I could pay off the war debt.

Alexei Please, Tom, for me this a serious thing. I try not to . . . mmm, sin?

Tom Sin?

Alexei Yes. Maybe it will surprise you, but I try to follow the words of God.

Tom You're a believer?

Alexei It is still possible in Soviet Union. Very difficult, and I must be always careful. It is not good for me if superiors know this.

Tom You go to church?

Alexei When possible. But it must be a little bit secret. And there are not so many since the last years. The government does not like. Many churches very old and very poor, bad condition of building. In Moscow, the church of my grandmother, before war, men come to . . . mmm, destroy it officially . . .

Tom Demolish . . .

Alexei Yes, and in that place they build a public toilet.

Tom They should have just converted it. Church and

cottage under one roof. My idea of Heaven.

Alexei Please, Tom, do not laugh. I think you should respect the beliefs of people, even if you are atheist.

Tom I'm no more an atheist than you, Alexei.

Alexei But then there is a big contradiction to be a man of your kind and to believe in God.

Tom *I've* never seen one. But then, of course, I am very High Church.

Alexei I hope that we will still be friends. I like you, Tom.

Tom Of course. No question.

Alexei I look forward to London very much.

Tom And I look forward to seeing you there.

Alexei I wish to ask a question.

Tom Yes?

Alexei First I must decide to trust you.

Tom Why shouldn't you?

Alexei I do not offend you, I hope, but is it true that you were a member of the Communist Party?

Tom How did you know that?

Alexei There are people here with much information about many things.

Tom It is true, yes, I *was*.

Alexei Ah.

Tom I joined when I was at school. But they've thrown me out now.

Alexei Why?

36

Tom I was rather critical of your great leader chumming up with Hitler in '39.

Alexei And now? You have not too much sympathy with Soviet Union?

Tom Look, I assure you, Alexei, that anything you ask me will be in complete confidence. Like the confessional.

Tom suddenly looks around the room.

Alexei It is safe. You are thinking about microphones?

Tom It suddenly crossed my mind.

Alexei There is nothing in this room.

Tom You're very sure.

Alexei Believe me. I know absolutely.

Tom Well, then.

Alexei I will be very frank.

Tom About what?

Alexei About asking advice.

Tom What sort of advice?

Alexei As example, if someone from my country was working in London and this person liked very much to stay, but is ordered to return to Soviet Union, is it possible that he stays?

Tom I imagine that would depend very much on what his work was.

Alexei If, as example, this person was working for, perhaps, Military Intelligence . . .

Tom As opposed to, say, press liaison . . .

Alexei As example, yes. How easy will it be for him to

make contact with some person who can help?

Tom You mean if he wanted to betray his country?

Alexei I mean, Tom, if his conscious, no . . .

Tom Conscience.

Alexei Yes. If his conscience is telling him that many things are not good in Europe, in east of Europe. He is an intelligent man and sees many bad things to happen in the next years.

Tom I think he should find a good friend who might have some contacts in the right places.

Alexei It is good advice, I think.

Tom We all need friends. Of different kinds.

Alexei You will help me?

Tom I can put you in touch with the right people.

Alexei Thank you, Tom.

Tom Are you quite sure about this?

Alexei I have considered this most carefully. And it is not betrayal, I think. (*He looks at Stalin.*) Betrayal is by him and the other similar people. They forget the truth, they forget the ideals. My father is like this also. In 1917 he was much involved and then, after, he was helping to change the old ways.

Tom Was he a soldier?

Alexei A scientist. Of, mmm . . . сельское хозяйство [agriculture] . . . it is to make best way to grow food, on farms and so on.

Tom An agricultural scientist?

Alexei Yes, he helped the people to grow good food, and

much more food. Because he believed in our Revolution, in the good things that came from it.

Tom And now?

Alexei Now he is not a scientist really. Yes, he is called a scientist, he works in high position, but it is all crazy. It is official science, proletarian science. This says there is nothing that cannot be changed by correct use of theory of Marx and Lenin. Everything is what it is because of . . . conditions, circumstance. So nature has not any mystery now. Nature of humans or nature of potatoes, as example. My father changes spring to winter, and winter to spring. 'Good morning, potato seeds, yesterday was such a cold winter, yes?'. . . because yesterday he reduces heating . . . and now he turns much electric light on . . . 'But today, potatoes, look, spring is arrived, so you must grow up quickly like good Socialist potatoes.'

Tom Does it work, though?

Alexei He tells me yes. But still the people have not enough to eat. It makes me sad for my country and for my father.

Tom I can't promise that your . . . offer will be accepted.

Alexei I know, Tom, but you will please try. It is very kind of you to help me. And perhaps in London sometimes I will not be so much on my guard for . . . surprises . . . fun.

Tom Despite your religious scruples?

Alexei Please?

Tom Alexei, I will help you because it's the right thing to do.

Alexei Just for this reason?

Tom Well, one's motives are never entirely unmixed, I suppose.

Kitty enters.

Kitty I'm not interrupting anything, I hope. Мы должы поторопиться. [We've got to get a move on. There's a special briefing tomorrow morning.]

Alexei Зачєм? [Why?]

Kitty Я не знаю. Мне только что сообщили. Поэтому, сегодня вечером нам нужно всё приготовить. [I don't know. I've just been told. So we'll have to get things ready tonight.]

Alexei Crazy, these people.

Alexei starts preparing the room, paying special attention to the table. He straightens the tablecloth and takes from a box various items to arrange on the table: notepads, pencils, ashtrays, table flags (three clusters, each with the Soviet, US and British flags) and lastly two stencilled name boards to be placed facing front in their respective places ('Generalissimo J. V. Stalin', 'President Harry S. Truman'). Kitty helps as she talks to Tom.

Kitty Big flap on. There's a briefing in the morning, suddenly, out of the blue.

Tom About what?

Kitty Search me. They're all being very hush-hush. Something big. All I know is we've got to be ready for 0900. *And* there's the reception tonight.

Tom I didn't tell you – I'm invited. By the Prime Minister.

Kitty Make sure you behave yourself.

Tom Whatever can you mean?

Kitty There'll be drink and there'll be soldiers. Don't get too bacchanalian.

Tom As if I would.

Alexei has picked up Clem's book from the table.

Alexei Well, well, surprise.

Kitty What?

Alexei Whose book?

Tom Oh, it's the Prime Minister's.

Alexei It is Lord Wyemsey book.

Kitty Wimsey.

Alexei Yes.

Tom So it is. *Five Red Herrings*. Well, I never.

Alexei It is first book from her I read. Lord Wimsey goes to Scotland and then he must to solve murder of artist, Mr Campbell. It is big mystery because . . .

Kitty It sounds fascinating, but could we get on?

Alexei Yes, yes. To read same book as your Prime Minister. I like this. Where is name?

Kitty What?

Alexei Name sign for Prime Minister.

Kitty Oh Lord, no. Are the stencils still there?

Alexei Please?

Kitty Трафарет. [Stencils].

Alexei looks in the box.

Alexei Да. [Yes].

Kitty Would you go to the office then, please, and get the paint and a brush?

Alexei Yes, I go.

Alexei exits.

Tom How long will he be?

Kitty Missing him already?

Tom Seriously.

Kitty A couple of minutes. Why?

Tom Do you have any intelligence connections, Kitty?

Kitty If I did, Tom, I probably shouldn't tell you. Why do you ask?

Tom That young man is not quite what he seems.

Kitty Oh?

Tom For a start he understands English rather better than he's been letting on. Which does have its funny side, I must admit.

Kitty Why?

Tom Think of some of the things you've said in front of him.

Kitty I mean, why has he been pretending?

Tom Orders. He claims to be Military Intelligence.

Kitty Alexei.

Tom You know he's being posted to their London embassy?

Kitty Don't I just? He's terribly excited about it.

Tom The thing is, he wants to get in touch with me when he's there to arrange a meeting with our cloak-and-dagger brigade.

Kitty With a view to . . . ?

Tom Coming over to us, I assume. He seems to be very disillusioned.

Kitty Seems to be?

Tom I'm not as green as I'm cabbage looking, Kitty. I don't want to drop myself in it if he's a phoney.

Kitty Why would he approach you?

Tom That's what I asked myself. I'm not unaware of my potential susceptibility to certain pressures.

Kitty I think you're wise to be cautious, Tom. An MP now. Caesar's wife and all that.

Tom Quite.

Kitty What did you say to him?

Tom I've told him yes. I do know people in London.

Kitty But you'd like me to take some soundings here first?

Tom I don't want to get out of my depth.

Kitty I'll see what I can find out for you.

Tom Discreetly, though, Kitty.

Kitty If the right person happens to be around this evening, I can probably let you know then.

Tom Thanks. Oh, why is life so complicated?

Kitty I thought you liked a complicated life.

Tom I suppose I do, really. Sometimes, though, there's something enormously attractive about . . . simple choices. That's the war for you, I suppose. Survive or perish. Freedom or conquest.

Kitty Yes. Everything becomes black or white, doesn't it?

Tom And when you've peered into the blackest black . . .

Kitty Yesterday?

Tom Christ, Kitty, you've no idea. Unspeakable.

Kitty Are you all right? (*She pours him a drink.*) Here. You're very pale.

Tom Thanks. Silly.

Kitty No.

Tom Better now.

Kitty Perhaps you should give the reception a miss. Have an early night.

Tom God, no. Not for the world.

Kitty You're in shock, if you ask me. Delayed shock.

Tom Balls.

Kitty Tom.

Tom I'm not giving up the chance of mingling with this lot at close quarters. I'd never forgive myself. Nor would my editor. Stop fussing, woman.

Kitty Thank you.

She resumes tidying the room.

Tom I'm sorry. I apologize.

Kitty Yes, well.

Tom Can I give you a hand?

Kitty No, thank you.

Tom wanders to the window and looks out.

Tom Oh, he's gone.

Kitty Who?

Tom That GI who was washing the President's car.

Kitty The very tall one? In tight trousers?

Tom Oh, you noticed him too?

Kitty He does rather stand out.

Tom Kitty!

Kitty I didn't mean that. Well . . . perhaps. I met him just now, on my way back here. He was lost, looking for the gents.

Tom Really? I must pay a little visit myself, actually.

Kitty Tom, no. You wouldn't.

Tom What?

Kitty Don't act the innocent. Anyway, judging from the look he gave my legs, he doesn't bat for your team.

Tom I think I understand cricket rather better than you.

Tom moves to the door.

Kitty There'll be tears before bedtime if you're not careful.

Tom I'm not in a careful mood.

Kitty You won't get anywhere with him.

Tom Bet?

Kitty Don't be disgusting. Five shillings then.

Tom You're on.

Tom exits. Kitty picks up the phone.

Kitty *(to phone)* Three two, please . . . Thank you . . . It's Second Officer Birbeck, sir – could we have a chat? . . . No, better not. Your office in twenty minutes? . . . sir.

She rings off and resumes organizing the room. Alexei enters, carrying a small paint pot and brush.

Alexei Where is Tom?

Kitty He'll be back in a minute . . . or two.

Alexei You write name, please. I copy.

Alexei sits at the table to stencil the name on to a blank board, copying it from the piece of paper on which Kitty has written it.

Kitty There.

Alexei Ah, thank you. He is nice man, Tom. We have good talk.

Kitty It wasn't too convoluted for you?

Alexei Please?

Kitty Nothing.

Alexei You know him well, for long time?

Kitty Slightly, before the war. We worked for the same newspaper in London. And then he came out here to cover the conference and we got to know each other better.

Alexei He is famous man in England?

Kitty He has a certain reputation. Yes, he is very popular, very widely read. Always speaks his mind.

Alexei Yes, I see this.

Kitty And what do you like about him?

Alexei He is, I think, interesting. In one hand he can be serious, with much deep thought of war and life. He has, I think, very deep, mmm . . . душа [soul].

Kitty Soul.

Alexei Yes. And in other hand he can be, mmm . . . something like brave and like funny . . . I think he likes to make shock to people . . . he is возмутительно [outrageous, flamboyant].

Kitty Oh, 'outrageous' . . . 'flamboyant'.

Alexei Flamboyant. Is nice sound, this word.

Outside the window we hear cars arriving. Alexei goes to look out.

Alexei Here comes *my* gong.

Kitty Gang.

Alexei Gang, yes. Gromyko . . . Molotov . . . Vishinsky . . . ah, Stalin.

Kitty How does he look?

Alexei Serious today. Not at all flamboyant.

Kitty I hope he's not going to be too much of a crosspatch. I suppose he's missing Mr Churchill. They did get on rather well. Oh, Lord . . .

Alexei What?

Kitty Mr Churchill's picture. It's still on the landing where we dumped it.

Alexei It is obstructing?

Kitty It doesn't look very nice, does it? It was bad enough the Prime Minister having to see it like that. Let's get it back to the office, before we have to cart it through in front of everyone else.

Alexei I have not finish this.

Kitty Do it later.

They are starting to leave as Tom enters.

47

Tom Another flap on?

Kitty A minor one, yes. No time to chat.

Tom Oh, Kitty . . .

Kitty Yes?

Tom You owe me two and ninepence.

Kitty and Alexei exit. Tom picks up the plate of rice pudding, and starts to eat.

Lights down.

Act Two

Late evening, the same day. The room is not yet completely tidy: the step ladder remains, as does the pot of paint. Clem's name board has been stencilled and reads 'C. R. Attlee'. The lights are off, but moonlight through the window shows Clem (now dressed in a dinner jacket with a medal ribbon) standing smoking his pipe and looking out. He holds a glass of brandy. The door opens and Kitty enters, turning on the lights.

Kitty Oh, I'm so sorry, Prime Minister.

Clem Quite all right.

Kitty I was expecting to find Mr Driberg.

Clem Saw him ten minutes ago, heading for the gentlemen's lavatory.

Kitty Ah.

Clem Think he might have partaken a little too freely of the hospitality. Certainly in a hurry to get there.

Kitty Indeed, sir.

Clem What *are* those flowers?

Kitty Sir?

Clem That huge display in the courtyard, the red star.

Kitty It is rather impressive, isn't it? They're geraniums.

Clem Geraniums. We had them in Putney.

Kitty Putney?

Clem Family home, as was. Good large garden. I always liked the geraniums.

Kitty Are there any at Downing Street?

Clem Didn't see any when they showed us round.

Kitty Perhaps you should have some put in, sir.

Clem I wouldn't want to put anyone to any trouble.

Kitty I'm sure you'd only have to ask, Prime Minister.

Clem Do you think so? Well, we'll see.

Kitty Can I bring you something? Another brandy?

Clem Thank you, no. How's it going on down there?

Kitty It's getting a little boisterous. Lots more toasts, and Mr Truman's started playing the piano.

Clem Oh dear.

Kitty Rather well, actually. Mr Stalin was clapping along like nobody's business.

Clem I suppose they have to let off steam somehow. Big decisions. Monumental. The Foreign Secretary's all right, is he? Not getting too argumentative?

Kitty Animated, I'd say. Talking to Mr Molotov when I last saw him. He *did* put the waiter into a bit of a tizzy earlier.

Clem Waiter?

Kitty He asked for a bottle of newts at dinner. Rather flummoxed his translator. It turned out he meant '*nuits*'. He wanted a bottle of Nuits-St-Georges.

Clem Newts. He's a wonderful man, Ernie. Very lucky to have him. No one's been asking after me?

Kitty Not that I'm aware, sir.

Clem As long as I get back for the 'goodnights'. Only courteous. They won't miss me till then.

Kitty You don't want to hear the orchestra, sir? They're just starting to set up.

Clem I don't think so.

Kitty Terribly natty costumes. They play balalaikas, I gather.

Clem Definitely not.

Kitty Mr Stalin had them brought over specially. It's just showing off, really. The Americans started it. The Russians had a pianist at the opening dinner, so the Americans had to go one better. They had a pianist and a violinist. So the Russians got in a string quartet. And then it was a ten-piece jazz band from the Americans. Lord knows what their response will be to the balalaikas.

Clem Doesn't do for me. All that noise, chatter. I dare say the Prime Minister enjoyed it.

Kitty The Prime Minister, sir?

Clem Can't quite get out of the habit yet.

Kitty Mr Churchill loved the chatter but hated the music. Though he did have the RAF band flown in for his first dinner – as a sort of revenge. 'The Skye Boat Song' and 'Mexican Serenade' at full military blast.

Clem You miss him, I imagine.

Kitty It does feel a little strange.

Clem Natural, after the last few years. I only hope he doesn't take it as ingratitude.

Kitty Sir?

Clem It's not. The people *are* grateful. But things had to change.

Kitty Speaking for myself, I don't think we could have come through without him. We'll always be in his debt for that.

Clem Yes, indeed.

Kitty But peace is different. Which is why I voted for you, sir.

Clem We had a lot of support from the Forces. Most pleasing.

Kitty It took the war, though, for me.

Clem May I ask why?

Kitty I think it's as simple as just meeting people, serving with them. The sort of people I'd never have met before, from places I'd scarcely heard of, and backgrounds . . . conditions I found hard to believe at first. But the more I found out, the more I realized that the Tories just haven't delivered the goods, after all the years they've had to do it. And all these people, my . . . comrades, I suppose, were still fighting and dying and showing the most extraordinary bravery, some of them, for a country which has failed them. And I thought, why should they go home to that same rottenness? Why should *I*? I cherish my country, I love it, and I want it to be a fair sort of place now. I suppose it boils down to bread for all before cake for some.

Clem Won't be easy, you know. But worth it.

From outside the window we hear indistinct shouting and then laughter. Clem goes over to look out.

Someone flat out on the steps. The sentries are hauling him up now. It looks like Stalin!

Kitty joins him at the window.

No, it's not, of course.

They turn away.

Kitty Oh, they've gone back in. I thought I caught a glimpse of a British uniform.

Clem Hope not.

Kitty Just high spirits, I think.

Clem Won't do if it *was* one of our chaps. Never have stood for it in my regiment. I'd have had him on a charge before his feet could touch.

Kitty May I ask, sir, what the medal is?

Clem Nothing much. Gallipoli.

Kitty What for?

Clem Oh . . . eating more bully-beef than anyone else, I expect. Is it me, or is it insufferably hot?

Kitty It *is* very close, isn't it?

Clem Most unpleasant.

Kitty I could bring you some water, sir, or a nice jug of lemon squash?

Clem Don't bother, thank you.

Kitty No bother, sir.

Clem No, no.

Clem pushes a cuff back and examines his wrist.

I think I've been bitten.

Kitty Mosquitoes, Prime Minister. There's masses of them. It's being so close to the lake.

Clem Itchy.

Kitty Horrid, aren't they?

He wanders over to the window and looks out.

Clem It is beautiful, though, the lake. And the woods.

Kitty Especially in the moonlight.

Clem Seems to have escaped the worst of the bombing.

Kitty The palace is completely untouched.

Clem Wonderful creepers. Reminds me of Oxford.

The door opens and Tom enters. He is wearing a novelty mask of Stalin and a Red Army cap. He addresses Kitty, oblivious of Clem, who is still by the window.

Tom Ninotchka! Come to your Uncle Joe.

Kitty Tom!

Tom The mass trials have been great success. There are now fewer but better Russians.

Kitty Tom.

Tom takes off the mask.

Tom I got it from a GI. They're all the rage in America.

He sniffs the air.

God, doesn't it linger, that dreadful bloody pipe?

He notices Clem, who walks to the door.

Clem I must just pop along the corridor to the, er . . .

Tom Prime Minister.

Clem exits.

Oh.

Kitty Yes, 'oh'.

Tom Bang go my chances of Number Eleven.

The phone rings. Kitty answers.

Kitty Press room . . . Да. Да. Нєт. Я понимаю. [Yes . . . yes . . . no . . . I understand.] Cathedral? Да. Я постараюсь сделать всё, что могу . . . до свидания. [Yes . . . I'll see what I can do . . . Goodbye.]

She rings off.

That was the guardroom. Whilst sending fraternal greetings and fully cognizant of the excellent relations subsisting between our two nations after their historic victory in the Patriotic War, sentry Protopopov (Order of Lenin, third class) would like his cap back.

Tom Or?

Kitty Or there will be unpleasantness which will make the battle of Stalingrad look like a picnic in a cathedral. I think it's the closest he could get to a vicarage tea party, but you get the drift.

Tom No sense of humour, that's their trouble.

Kitty Don't sulk. Now, about Alexei. I've had a word with someone. The first thing to be sure of is that he's worth the trouble, that he is what he claims to be.

Tom Not just a glorified office boy who sees the chance of a life in the decadent West?

Kitty And who might turn out to be a considerable embarrassment . . . to an MP with a specific predilection.

She produces an envelope which she hands to Tom.

Now, if he *is* Military Intelligence, he'll apparently know the answers to these questions off the top of his head.

Tom God, Kitty, I said be discreet. I can't start interrogating him.

Kitty It's nothing high grade, they said, just general stuff to establish his *bona fides*. Get him to write down the answers and then you bring them to me.

Tom He won't like it.

Kitty That's the way it's done, according to my connection. I'm afraid he doesn't have a choice. It is in your interest, Tom.

Tom Yes, I know. I'll try. Where will you be?

Kitty Boogying away to the hep rhythms of Vasily Bupnov and his Balalaika Vagabonds. After I've averted a diplomatic incident.

She picks up the uniform cap and exits as Alexei enters.

Alexei Tom, what do you want? I must not be for too long away from the reception.

Tom It's about our conversation earlier.

Alexei You have not changed your mind?

Tom No, quite the reverse. I've set things in motion.

Alexei Please?

Tom I've already spoken to someone about you.

Alexei Now?

Tom Yes.

Alexei Who?

Tom That doesn't matter.

Alexei But I tell you these things in secret. You say it is

56

like confessional. In London you speak to contact, not here.

Tom Well, I have.

Alexei Why, Tom? This is dangerous for me.

Tom It's not entirely without complications for me. I'm sure you understand that, Alexei, as a Military Intelligence officer.

Alexei You do not have trust in me.

Tom It's not that, but I must protect my position.

Alexei I am not happy with this.

Tom It's done now.

Alexei And how is the answer from your contact?

Tom They would like some information from you.

Alexei Now? Information? No, no, this is too soon, Tom. It is crazy.

Tom Don't get into such a tiz. They're not after the colour of Stalin's drawers. Just enough to show them you're what you say you are.

Tom produces the envelope.

Alexei I know what I am.

Tom Yes, but they have to be sure.

Alexei *You* believe me?

Tom Of course I believe you.

Alexei Show to me.

Tom hands him the envelope, which he opens to take out a single sheet of typewritten paper. He studies it in silence.

Tom Well?

Alexei I know this information. They are not important things.

Tom You see.

Alexei I am not still happy with this situation.

Tom It's the only way, I'm afraid.

Alexei Your Parker, please. And this time, not to drop it.

Tom hands him the pen and he writes. Tom wanders over to the window and looks out. Alexei folds the paper, replaces it in the envelope and hands it to Tom.

There.

Tom Thank you.

Alexei I hope I do not make mistake.

Tom You said you knew the answers.

Alexei To do this for you, I mean.

Tom I'm sure it's the right thing.

Alexei And what now?

Tom I'll take this back to . . . my contact, and see what they say.

Tom moves towards the door. Alexei makes to follow.

No, you stay here. I'll come back.

Alexei I must return before too long.

Tom What's the hurry?

Alexei I am required to assist translator to Comrade Molotov. She is not so experienced, this translator, and has much difficulty with your Mr Bevin.

Tom His accent?

Alexei Vocabulary more. Tom, what exactly means 'bunch of fives matey'?

Tom As in?

Alexei Mmm . . . 'You are talking like someone who wants a bunch of fives matey.'

Tom Well, I suppose . . . 'Your words demonstrate that you are a man who wants . . . to show great understanding, my friend.' Roughly. It's very idiomatic.

Alexei Good. Thank you.

Tom But do stay here for the moment. I won't be long.

Alexei You promise this?

Tom Yes.

Tom exits. Alexei picks up Clem's book and stands flipping through the pages, being careful not to disturb the bookmark near the end. Clem enters. Alexei straightens to attention.

Clem Ah.

Alexei Prisypkin. Captain.

Clem Attlee. Prime Minister. That's my book.

Alexei Yes, *Five Red Herrings*. I have not disturbed your place in it.

Clem I should hope not.

Alexei I apologize, Prime Minister, but for me it is a big excitement that you also read about Lord Wimsey.

Clem Ah, *you* do then?

Alexei Yes, I am big fan for Dorothy L. Sayers.

Clem She is good, isn't she?

Alexei This is her first book I read.

Clem In English?

Alexei In Russian translation first. Then later in English. But slowly.

Clem Do stand easy.

Alexei Please?

Clem No need to stay like that.

Alexei Ah, yes. Thank you. (*He relaxes.*)

Clem Which is your favourite?

Alexei I like very much *Nine Tailors*.

Clem Excellent, yes.

Alexei And *Clouds of Witness*.

Clem Not one of her best, I don't think.

Alexei Perhaps. *Murder Must Advertise*?

Clem That one I don't know.

Alexei I can recommend.

Clem Ah. Well, I'm almost on my last chapter. Due for a new read.

Alexei You will like, I think. Many very flamboyant characters.

Clem Oh.

Alexei But my favourite is always, I think, *Five Red Herrings*.

Clem Because it was your first one, I expect.

Alexei Of course, yes. But more. First because I like to read about Scotland. Very beautiful place, I think. And second, I like that there are so many, mmm . . . suspects, yes, who had possibility to kill Mr Campbell.

Clem Six of them, yes. Hence five red herrings.

Alexei Yes. And at first I think guilty man is Mr Farren.

Clem Because of that odd business with the bicycle?

Alexei At Kirk-cud-bright. Yes.

Clem Kircudbright.

Alexei Please?

Clem That's how it's pronounced.

Alexei Ah. You are sure?

Clem Yes.

Alexei Ah. Thank you.

Clem I've worked out that Strachan must have pinched Farren's bicycle . . . stolen it.

Alexei Yes, of course. But this is not significant information. Lord Peter is more clever. It is the train to Glasgow that is significant. The watch of Mr Ferguson has stopped, yes? So he is too late for that train he tells he is on. In fact, he was on later train and so must to mmm . . . forge, yes, the clipping of his ticket.

Clem Ferguson?

Alexei Yes. And when Lord Peter understands this, very brilliant, he knows that Ferguson finds his watch has stopped *after* he killed Mr Campbell. But he only understands this . . . ah . . . in last chapter . . . which is chapter you have not read, I am sorry. I apologize.

61

Clem What's your name again?

Alexei Prisypkin. I am sorry, Prime Minister.

Clem First name?

Alexei Alexei. It was stupid. I am sorry.

Clem opens the book, takes a pen, inscribes the flyleaf and hands it to Alexei.

Clem Souvenir of Potsdam.

Alexei Thank you. I apologize again.

Clem Don't mention it. Not important.

Alexei You are very kind, understanding. You are talking like someone who wants a bunch of fives matey. I mean this sincerely.

The phone rings. Alexei answers it.

(*to phone*) Hallo . . . Да, у телефона . . . да, Бевин, да. [Yes, speaking . . . Yes, Bevin, yes.] 'Monkey'? Mmm, monkey . . . Нет, нет. Подождите. [No, no, it's gone. Hang on.] (*to Clem*) Forgive, Prime Minister, but please to tell me what are 'monkeys'?

Clem Monkeys? They're animals.

Alexei Animals?

Clem Yes, they live in trees.

Alexei In trees?

Clem Yes. Monkeys, you know.

Alexei Please, I do not know, which is why I ask.

Clem Monkeys.

Clem performs a brief and reluctant monkey impersonation.

Alexei Ah. Обезьяны. [Monkeys]. You are sure?

Clem Quite sure.

Alexei Thank you. *(to phone)* 'Обезьяны'. Да . . . Я сейчас спущусь. ['Monkeys'. Yes . . . I will come down.] *(He rings off.)* I must to return, for problem with translator. Please, if Mr Tom Driberg comes, you will tell him I am here. Not now, but later.

Clem Certainly.

Alexei And thank you, Prime Minister, for the book.

  He reads the inscription.

'*You* might as well have this now. C. R. Attlee.' It will be great treasure for me.

Clem Good.

Alexei 'Monkeys'. I still do not understand.

Clem Yes, well, I don't think I can help you any more.

Alexei Of course, I go. 'As for Mr Molotov's Vienna proposal, Mr Bevin does not give a monkey's.' Strange. But it is a challenge, yes? Goodbye.

  Alexei exits. Clem picks up the phone and waits for the switchboard.

Clem *(to phone)* Yes, Attlee. Can you put me through to my Mr Elyot. He's at the reception . . . Thank you . . . Elyot? . . . Call off Ernie, would you, from Molotov . . . he'll lose us Austria.

  He notices a copy of The Times *lying with some not yet cleared rubbish. He picks it up and settles down to do the crossword, filling his pipe from a tobacco pouch. Tom enters.*

Tom Oh, Prime Minister.

Clem Driberg.

Tom Crossword.

Clem Yes.

Tom Concise?

Clem Cryptic.

Tom You're not tempted downstairs by the jollities?

Clem Quite happy here.

Tom Ah, good. Have you seen Captain Prisypkin, by any chance?

Clem Just talking to him. Interesting young chap. Do you intend going down there?

Tom I beg your pardon, Prime Minister?

Clem Back downstairs.

Tom Oh, I see.

Clem Only I think he wants you to wait here.

Tom Thank you, sir.

Clem prepares to light his pipe.

Clem No objection?

Tom Of course not, Prime Minister. Perhaps it will keep the mosquitoes at bay. I really must apologize for earlier.

Clem Not at all.

Tom I was, perhaps, a little over-exuberant. With the mask.

Clem How's the original behaving?

Tom He's conducting the orchestra, much to their alarm. They don't know *what* to do – half of them are following him and the other half are just pretending. Dreadful noise.

Clem Better off here, then.

Tom About this briefing in the morning, sir. Any hints?

Clem No.

Tom Of course. Sorry.

Clem 'Eleven inches'. Very nice.

Tom Sir?

Clem 'Team moves slowly about twenty-eight centimetres.' Must be. You do them?

Tom Crosswords? No. Desperately dull, I'm afraid, for me.

Clem They keep the old brainbox ticking over, I find.

Tom Too . . . ordered, neat. There's only ever the one solution.

Clem You surprise me.

Tom Why?

Clem I would have thought that was the attraction.

Tom Order? Neatness?

Clem A reflection of your political views, surely?

Tom I'm afraid you've lost me, Prime Minister.

Clem A finite problem. Only one correct solution. Marx and Lenin.

Tom Hardly the same.

Clem You don't see it?

Tom No, I don't. Of course Socialist theory offers a solution. That's what a theory's for. But it doesn't have to be dull. Not if it's informed by passion. Marx and Lenin didn't conjure up their ideas as the answer to a puzzle, an intellectual challenge. They had hearts that beat with indignation, with a longing for justice.

Clem Yes, yes, yes. We all come to Socialism through our hearts. Pretty bad show if we didn't.

Tom Even you, sir?

Clem Meaning?

Tom No disrespect, Prime Minister, but my impression is of a man not prone to demonstrativeness. Of a cerebral cast of mind.

Clem No disrespect there. I was walking in the East End. Newly qualified barrister, silk hat, tail coat, must have looked a regular dandy. A young girl fell into step beside me, as children do. Seven, eight years old. Pale, thin, dirty, ragged, barefoot. Bitterly cold day. She asked where I was going. I said, 'I'm going home to have my tea. Where are *you* going?' She said, 'I'm going home to see if there *is* any tea.' Profoundly moving. Heart, do you see?

Tom Yes.

Clem After the heart, though, it's the brain that has to make sense of it all.

Tom But without sacrificing passion, surely?

Clem As long as it's kept under control.

Tom But why?

Clem Balance. An essentially British quality, don't you think?

Tom Compromise.

Clem Nothing wrong with that, if it's for the general good.

Tom Principles, though.

Clem Our principles are sound.

Tom Let's act on them then. We have a clear mandate. We must listen to the people. *They're* passionate for a just society, equality.

Clem Nothing to lose but their chains?

Tom Still holds true.

Clem Stuff and nonsense. Many would have a great deal to lose. If we go at it like a bull in a china shop we'll have galloping inflation. How will that serve the retired teacher who can't manage on her pension? Or the foundryman who finds his Post Office savings book isn't worth the paper it's printed on? We must be cautious, trim to the wind.

Tom Where's the inspiration in that? The zeal?

Clem We won't go short with you around, I'm sure. In your column, or from the back benches.

Tom I'm not a voice in the wilderness, sir. Have you listened to the unions?

Clem I always listen to the unions. They're our backbone. But we are a national party now. We will not represent purely sectional interests. That was our mistake in the past. And we paid dearly for it.

Tom At least we had our fervour.

Clem Fervour? As in 'religious'?

Tom Why not? It is a transforming experience, coming to Socialism – for me at any rate. Seeing the light, you might say.

Clem You're Catholic?

Tom Anglo, yes. Why?

Clem It shows. Dogma. Infallibility. Virtue, sin. Heaven, hell. Blessed, damned. No shades of grey.

Tom Not as far as absolute right's concerned, no.

Clem How can you ever be sure?

Tom Faith.

Clem Irrational.

Tom Some things are.

Clem 'Put off holiness, put on intellect.' Blake.

Tom You don't believe in Christianity?

Clem The ethics, yes. Can't stand the mumbo-jumbo.

Tom So you're an agnostic?

Clem Haven't made up my mind yet.

Tom laughs.

Why is that funny?

Tom Sorry, Prime Minister. But don't you believe in a scheme of things, a grand design?

Clem Religiously? Politically?

Tom Both, I suppose.

Clem You know, you're what I call a mosaic Socialist, Driberg. Correct me if I'm wrong, but you see society, a good Socialist society, as made up of lots and lots of little pieces all the same shape and size as each other, nothing in themselves; but arranged into a pattern, the design emerges as harmonious and pleasing.

Tom A jigsaw rather, I think. Different shapes and sizes, but yes, all having to fit together to produce the complete picture.

Clem For me, it's a garden. Harmonious and pleasing as you approach from a distance. And then, close up, you see that every plant is unique. Not only are they different shapes, sizes, colours, but they grow differently: faster or slower, better in the spring or in the autumn, in the light or in the shade. But they'll all thrive in their own way if they're well tended. A little judicious pruning sometimes, to maintain variety. There's even room for a few exotics. The point is, it's always changing. Each plant, and the garden itself, is in a state of becoming. When your jigsaw's finished, there's nothing left to do. The gardener's work is never done.

Tom I'm afraid I find it hard to be passionate about gardening. Jigsaws too, if it comes to that.

Clem You confuse passion with extravagance. Plenty of gardeners who'd admit to a passion, but they don't prance about the flower beds making a song and dance about it. They get on with the job.

Tom 'Prance', Prime Minister?

Clem No offence.

Tom Some taken, I'm afraid, sir.

Clem I do hear things.

Tom And?

Clem If you can't give it up, you should keep it quiet.

Tom I have tried . . . to keep it quiet.

Clem Yes, Beaverbrook *was* good to you.

Tom The court case? May I ask how much you know?

Clem Enough not to like what I heard, frankly. Miners, weren't they?

Tom God, no. One was at least thirty and the other was about twenty-five.

Clem Sorry?

Tom Unemployed miners down from Scotland. Yes, they did stop me near my flat at midnight and ask if I knew of any cheap lodgings; yes, I did invite them back to talk; yes, I was planning an article on unemployment in the coalfields; yes, I only have one bedroom and didn't want them stealing anything if they slept downstairs on the sofa; yes, we all slept in my huge huge bed; yes, I was accused of an attempted seduction; yes, I was found not guilty; and yes, Lord Beaverbrook managed to keep it out of the papers. I think that covers it.

Clem Won't do, you know.

Tom No room for exotics after all?

Clem If they're too showy they can unbalance the garden.

Tom Or the party?

Clem Advancement depends on more than talent.

Tom I would be advised to . . . modify my tastes?

Clem Behaviour.

Tom The act, not the intention?

Clem Theologically unsound, I grant you.

Tom Oh, I don't know. Eleventh commandment: 'Thou shalt not get found out.'

Clem Difficult though, for exotics to flourish in the shade.

Tom Can we please get out of the bloody garden? I'm sorry, but you'll be talking about pansies next. Pink ones, probably.

Clem Let's not be smutty.

Tom At least I now know where I stand in terms of my parliamentary career.

Clem I'm sure you'll do a good job, however far you rise.

Tom And my politics?

Clem We're a broad church.

Tom I won't compromise, sir, in my private life either.

Clem Is it such a bad word, 'compromise'? 'Promise together.' This conference is run on compromise, and it will make Europe a safer place. Waging war is full of compromise – or do you think it as simple a matter as good against evil? Life is a compromise, for goodness' sake. It's the duty of those of us called upon to serve to effect the best compromise, the one that serves the greater good. And the decisions aren't always easy.

Tom Good is good. Neither lesser nor greater.

Clem Do you know who you remind me of, Driberg? Those dreadful people who interrupt one's elevenses and preach at you on the doorstep, clutching their bibles and pamphlets. Not now, of course, my policeman would soon see them off. But there's that same refusal to brook any sort of argument, to consider even for a second that the other chap may have a worthwhile point of view. You've built a wall of total and utter certainty around yourself, and nothing, not even the most cogent and well-advanced argument, can make a chink in it. I'm talking politically now. I don't understand the other stuff you get up to, and frankly I'm happy to remain in a state of blessed ignorance. But those bible-bashers on the doorstep deflect any challenging question with a smug reference to Leviticus chapter four verse two in the same way as you and your people quote Marx and Lenin. The correct answer is always to be found in the scriptures. No matter what the question, it can be dealt with by a numbered paragraph. It's a *theology* of Marx and Lenin, not a theory. Absolute right or wrong. And if there is a dispute amongst the theologians, people suffer. You were in Spain, like me. You saw what happened when the left argued about how many angels could dance on the head of a pin. Socialist killed Socialist. They'd killed the priests – something, by the way, I'd have thought would have given you pause for thought – and then they turned on each other. Where was the good then, greater *or* lesser? And I know you liked the bravura and the excitement and the passion, but what I saw was the killing. And let me tell you, I had enough the last time. Terrible waste. But we served, we did our job. And yes, we all had to compromise. I certainly did. I had to threaten to kill one of my own men. He'd funked it, wouldn't go over the top. My pistol was steady, pointed straight at him, poor chap. And I'd have pulled the trigger – he was endangering the lives of the whole platoon. Greater good, do you see? So I had to set aside absolutism and prepare myself to take the life of a comrade. Didn't need to, as it turned out, thank God, but I was ready to. And that wasn't for theory or theology, it was for survival. There was no shouting of slogans, no waving of banners – although strangely enough, I did wave a red flag once, dodging the bullets, screaming at the top of my voice. It was the only way I could draw attention to the fact that my chaps were coming under fire from our own side. Sorry to disappoint you. You'd have thought better of me if it had been *your* sort of red flag, wouldn't you? A gesture. A symbol of a ferocious certainty. Like the armies of the popes with their beautifully wrought banners, trampling over the maimed bodies of non-believers, but exciting the passions of everyone else, gulling them into believing in absolute right or wrong. It's a cheap trick. Ours is a great party, a great movement, and no one person, no one grouping has a monopoly of commitment to justice. There will be no pope, certainly not me. I take as a compliment the things they say. Do you imagine I don't know how people see me? Do you think things never get back to me, one way or another? The clever little quips, polished in the tea room and passed around the Members' bar? 'Mr Attlee is a modest man' – 'Yes, he has much to be modest about.' 'An empty taxi drew up outside Number Ten and Mr Attlee got out.' 'A sheep in sheep's clothing.' Have *you* heard any good ones lately? I've marched behind banners, I've sung the fighting songs, we all have. But now we have the chance to serve, to make a real difference. We must know our limitations, our fallibilities. I can't sing songs any more. People would laugh if I did.

He starts to sing. By the end of the third verse he is standing on the table in front of his own portrait adopting an heroic pose.

> 'England arise! the long long night is over
> Faint in the east behold the dawn appear
> Out of your evil dream of toil and sorrow
> Arise, O England, for the day is here
> From your fields and hills
> Hark! the answer swells
> Arise, O England, for the day is here!
>
> By your young children's eyes so red with weeping
> By their white faces aged with want and fear
> By the dark cities where your babes are creeping
> Naked of joy and all that makes life dear
> From each wretched slum
> Let the loud cry come
> Arise, O England for the day is here!'

Tom Prime Minister . . .

Clem 'Forth then, ye heroes, patriots and lovers!
　　　Comrades of danger, poverty and scorn!
　　　Mighty in faith of Freedom, your great Mother!
　　　Giants refreshed in Joy's new-rising morn!
　　　Come and swell the song
　　　Silent now so long
　　　England is risen – and the day is here.'

Tom (*joins in the last line*) 'England is risen – and the day is here.'

Clem steps abruptly down from the table.

Clem You see. Doesn't suit. Me or the country.

Tom Perhaps because it's rather a dull hymn. Very Low Church.

Clem It doesn't reek of incense, thankfully, no. But at least it comes from our own tradition.

Tom Which achieved what? Dividend stamps with a pound of Co-op bacon, precious little else. A far cry from revolution.

Clem We'll have a revolution, but in our own way. Unextravagant. Without tears.

Tom A revolution without tears?

Clem They blur the vision.

The phone rings. Tom answers.

Tom (*to phone*) Hallo . . . yes, one moment. (*to Clem*) For you, sir . . .

Clem takes the phone.

Clem (*to phone*) Yes? . . . I see . . . Where? . . . When? . . . What's that our time? . . . Yes, immediately. (*He rings off.*) Must go, I'm afraid. Goodnights and all that.

He moves to the door.

Oh, Driberg, any talk of me standing on a table singing, I'll deny it.

Tom I wouldn't be believed anyway, Prime Minister.

Clem exits. Tom finds Clem's glass and drains the rest of the brandy. The phone rings. Tom answers.

Hallo, an English country garden, what can I do for you? . . . I don't understand, I'm afraid . . . English, I'm English . . . *Anglyski*, do you follow? . . . No, *niet*, try later.

He rings off. He notices the Stalin mask, picks it up, puts it on and leans out of the window waving. We hear a burst of laughter from the courtyard. Alexei enters.

Alexei Ah, Tom.

Tom turns back from the window.

Tom Comrade Prisypkin!

Alexei Take off, Tom. Take it off.

Tom All right, all right.

Tom removes the mask.

Alexei You think he is a joke for me? This man is not a joke. He is a . . . mmm, monster, yes? True monster.

Tom You have to laugh at monsters.

Alexei You understand nothing.

Tom I'm sorry. I didn't mean to upset you.

Alexei Well, maybe in London I can laugh at him.

Tom Ah, London. What will you want to see first in London?

Alexei Yes, mmm . . . British Museum, Buckingham Palace, National Gallery, Houses of Parliament, all these famous places. And Scotland, I like to go to Scotland. Perhaps I walk there, in the mountains, for holiday from London. Do you like to walk in hills, mountains, Tom? Good place for thinking, yes, for considering with yourself. And after, the head is more clear, yes? Things can seem to be better, to live can be good, mmm . . .

Tom Alexei, what's the matter?

Alexei Who did you tell about me?

Tom An intermediary. Someone who knows someone.

Alexei Kitty?

Tom Why?

Alexei Just now she is dancing with my superior, head of section. And I think they talk about me.

Tom So?

Alexei He has a way to look at people, when there is trouble. He looks at me this way.

Tom I'm sure not.

Alexei I know this was big mistake, for you to tell about me before London.

Tom Kitty wouldn't say anything. Why should she?

Alexei Ah, it *was* her you tell. I said not to, Tom.

Tom I think you're getting in a tiz about nothing.

Alexei I hope, yes. But I do not believe.

Tom produces a hip flask and offers it to Alexei.

Tom Don't be such a worry-boots. Here.

Alexei Thank you, no.

    Tom drinks.

Tom Oh, someone telephoned for you just now.

Alexei Who?

Tom I don't know. Russian. I just caught your name, that's all.

Alexei I have bad feeling, Tom.

    The phone rings. Alexei gestures to it.

Please.

    Tom answers it.

Tom (*to phone*) Hallo? . . . One moment.

    He holds the receiver out to Alexei, who takes it.

Alexei (*to phone*) Присыпкин . . . когда, товарищ командир? . . . есть, товарищ командир? . . . да, товарищ командир. [Prisypkin . . . When, sir? . . . Why, sir? . . . Yes, sir.] (*He rings off.*)

Tom What?

Alexei Head of section. I must to report urgently.

Tom Did he say why?

Alexei Just that I report now, immediately.

Tom It could be anything.

Alexei I can tell. His voice is serious. He must know, I think, about my intention.

Tom How could he, Alexei?

Alexei I am frightened, Tom.

Tom Just calm down. It's nothing, I'm sure.

Alexei You think?

Tom I do.

Alexei moves to the door.

Alexei Tom, if it *is* bad thing . . .

He breaks off as Kitty enters. Alexei exits.

Kitty Is he all right?

Tom He's got some idea that they know about his approach to us.

Kitty Who does?

Tom His section head.

Kitty Viktor? I was just tripping the light fantastic with him. As much as one can to a balalaika orchestra.

Tom Alexei said. And this Viktor didn't seem suspicious at all about Alexei?

Kitty He'd hardly tell me, would he, if he was? I don't see how he could be, though.

Tom It's just that he ordered Alexei to report to him pretty damn sharpish.

Kitty It could be for anything.

Tom That's what I said. I can take it, by the way, that our people are happy with him?

Kitty The answers to the questions were spot on, yes. He's certainly Military Intelligence.

Tom And genuine? Not playing some dreadfully intricate double game?

Kitty They have nothing on him to suggest that he's anything other than completely genuine.

78

Tom So perhaps I'm not such a bad judge of character after all.

Kitty You were wrong about Ulysses, though.

Tom Who?

Kitty The GI.

Tom Ulysses? How do you know his name?

Kitty He's taking me for a drive tomorrow evening. In the moonlight.

Tom Well.

Kitty And he's given me three pairs of very sheer nylons.

Tom Beware Greeks bearing gifts, that's all I have to say to you. And make sure you get the full five bob's worth.

Kitty I will. Was the Prime Minister up here with you all that time?

Tom Yes. Fascinating.

Kitty There's a big confab going on now with the three of them. About this briefing in the morning, I suppose. He didn't say anything to you about it?

Tom Very clam-like when I asked him.

Kitty Look at this room. I can't face finishing it tonight. What's that? (*noticing Clem's tobacco pouch on the table*)

Tom The Prime Ministerial tobacco.

Kitty I must take it down to him when I go. You rather put your foot in it there, didn't you?

Tom He didn't make anything of it.

Kitty What *did* you talk about?

Tom Gardening.

Kitty Oh, not geraniums, by any chance?

Tom Exotics. Kitty, do you think I'm too . . . ferociously certain all the time?

Kitty Just most of the time.

Tom But there's nothing wrong, is there, in sticking to one's guns if one knows one's right? I mean, it's all too easy to betray a principle.

Kitty Perhaps it's not the certainty but the ferocity that's concerning you. If that's what this is – concern.

Tom I'm not totally indifferent to the way others see me.

Kitty You're not mellowing in your old age, are you, Tom?

Tom Old age?

Kitty Well, middle age then.

Tom Thank you for reminding me.

Kitty What are friends for?

Tom Perhaps I should marry.

Kitty What?

Tom *You* wouldn't have me, would you?

Kitty Tom!

Tom No sex. Not with each other. A smart house, parties . . . companionship.

Kitty You've been up too long. So have I, come to that. I'd better go down before they all disappear, and find a volunteer to get up at the crack of dawn and help me make things shipshape.

Tom Alexei will, won't he?

Kitty Of course, yes. Silly.

Tom Kitty.

Kitty Will you turn out the light when you leave? What?

Tom Why won't Alexei be here to help you?

Kitty I didn't say he wouldn't.

Tom This is me.

Kitty You'll think it horrid. It *is*, I suppose. But try and take the long view.

Tom What's going on?

Kitty Alexei will not be coming to London.

Tom Why not?

Kitty He's no longer considered reliable.

Tom But you said they thought he was genuine.

Kitty You misunderstand. It's not us who don't consider him reliable.

Tom He was right, then? To be worried about Viktor?

Kitty They're taking him away tonight. On to Moscow tomorrow.

Tom How did they find out? (*Kitty's silence answers.*) For Christ's sake, why?

Kitty We have to take the long view.

Tom You betrayed him.

Kitty An apparent indiscretion on the dance floor. Enough to make them wonder, that's all.

Tom Why, though? If he's genuine?

Kitty We . . . that is, our people, happen to know who

would be in line to replace him in London. And this person is of rather more use to us than Alexei would be. I can't tell you why, but please understand that there *are* degrees of usefulness in this sort of thing. Alexei is very low grade.

Tom You seem to know a great deal about it. For someone in your position.

Kitty Just because the fighting's over, that doesn't mean there's not a war. Of sorts.

Tom How could you? You must know what will happen to him.

Kitty If he holds out, he might convince them that they're wrong.

Tom And if not?

Kitty I am sorry, really.

Tom Balls. That's not good enough.

Tom moves to the door.

Kitty Where are you going?

Tom To find him, warn him.

Kitty I don't think you should.

Tom I'm under nobody's orders. I'll do what the hell I please.

Kitty There's nowhere for him to go. And if he's observed having a tête-à-tête with you, it will just confirm their suspicions.

Tom Which you so charmingly aroused.

Kitty I am still a serving officer who has the interests of her country at heart. As have you, I'm sure.

Tom I'll never forgive you for this.

Kitty Well, it *is* for the best, you know, not to tell him now. It would just frighten him earlier than necessary.

Tom Such consideration.

Kitty I do understand. You were rather fond of him, weren't you?

Tom Of course I wasn't. I just wanted to suck his cock.

Kitty Tom!

Tom Why don't you get out?

Alexei enters, cap on, briefcase in hand.

Alexei Ah, good. You are here still. I come to say goodbye. I must return to Moscow.

Tom Yes, I'm sorry.

Alexei You know?

Kitty Viktor told me.

Alexei It is bad news for me. But perhaps not too serious. He is strong man.

Tom Who?

Alexei My father.

Tom I don't understand.

Alexei Ah, you think I must go for what we talked about before? No. You were right, Tom, it was nothing bad. Well, that sounds unkind. Of course it is bad. My father has problem with his heart and asks to see me.

Tom Oh. You've spoken to him?

Alexei No, he is in hospital. But they send message from him. And Viktor, very kind, gives permission for me. He

. . . mmm, pulls some string, this is correct expression? Tom?

Tom Spot on, yes.

Alexei He pulls some string to get me place on transport plane which leaves in morning.

Tom I do so hope everything will be all right, that you won't arrive to bad news.

Kitty We mustn't be pessimistic, Tom. I'm sure Alexei would prefer . . . to travel hopefully. It's a long journey.

Alexei Yes, and they wait for me now, so . . . until London.

Tom Yes.

Alexei Oh, I forget. I have your address, but not telephone number.

He produces the notebook page from his pocket and feels for a pen. Tom produces his Parker.

Tom Here.

Tom takes the page, writes on it, and gives it back to Alexei with the pen.

Please. Keep it.

Alexei Really?

Tom Of course.

Alexei Thank you, Tom, thank you. This is wonderful. Souvenir of Potsdam. Of you.

They embrace.

Tom Goodbye, Alexei.

Kitty I'll come down and see you off.

Alexei Thank you. Goodbye, Tom.

Kitty and Alexei exit. Tom picks up the phone.

Tom (*to phone*) Yes, can you get me London? . . . it's
Fleet double two two nine . . . thank you.

*He rings off. We hear the sound of a car starting. Doors
slam and the car drives away. Clem enters.*

Clem Ah. Lost my shag.

Tom You too, Prime Minister?

Clem There it is. What? (*He picks up his tobacco pouch.*)
Are you all right, Driberg?

Tom Yes, of course.

Clem Enjoyed our little chat. You'll be at the briefing in
the morning?

Tom Yes, I'll be there.

Clem Goodnight then.

Tom Goodnight, sir.

Clem It all comes down to the greater good, believe me.

*Clem exits. The teleprinter starts to operate. Tom reads
the message but is interrupted by the phone, which he
answers.*

Tom Hallo? . . . Thank you . . . copy takers, Driberg . . .
Frank? What are *you* still doing there? Double shift? . . .
Yes, there's something on it coming through here now.
Where did they drop the thing? . . . Where the hell's that?
. . . Why not on Tokyo? . . . Hold on, would you, I'll see
what we've got . . .

*He goes to the teleprinter, tears off the message and
returns to the phone.*

Truman says 'America has harnessed the basic power of the universe' . . . typical Yank overstatement, I expect. Bigger and better and all that. Listen, Frank, can I get an extra para on my piece? . . . a hundred? That'll do. Begins 'To return from the hitherto undreamed-of world of that camp to the all too real world of this conference, where fudge and compromise and betrayal are in the very air, is to concentrate the mind on how we can best achieve our goals after this epoch-making election. Once there were . . .' Yes, I know. Look, do me a favour, would you, and just take it down as it sounds for the moment? 'Once there were principles, passions, symbols and songs. The principles remain, I think and I hope, but where is the passion, where are the songs, where are the symbols? Can there be a revolution without tears? Perhaps William Blake was right: "Exuberance is beauty. The road of excess leads to the palace of Wisdom."' . . . Frank? . . . Hallo? . . . bugger bugger bugger bugger bugger. No, I'm sorry, dear, not you . . . No, don't bother. It's really not that important.

He rings off. Outside we hear car doors slam, shouting, whistles and the departure of cars, motorbikes. The teleprinter starts operating again. Tom picks up the paint pot and brush, climbs the ladder and starts to paint Lenin's beard on to Clem's face.

Lights down.